Father tell me your story

This Book Belongs To

____

____

____

____

How did you feel when you found out that you were going to be a father?

Were you present for the birth of your child?

How did you feel at the birth of your child or at the first sight of your child?

What were your concerns when you brought your child/children home?

What do you like about being a Dad?

What do you not like about being a Dad?

What do you wish for your child?

What do you feel your role is as a Dad?

What do you teach your children about love?

What is your advice about relationships?

What do you teach your children about money?

Describe your relationship with your father.

How much time did your father spend with you?

How often did your father tell you that he loved you?

What did your father teach you about life?

What did your father teach you about love?

What did your father teach you about relationships?

What did your father do that made you happy?

What is your fondest memory of your father?

What did your father do that made you sad?

What do you wish you could tell your father?

Describe how you are like your father.

Describe your relationship with your mother.

How much time did your mother spend with you?

How often did your mother tell you that she loved you?

What did your mother teach you about life?

What did your mother teach you about love?

What did your mother teach you about relationships?

What did your mother do that made you happy?

What is your fondest memory of your mother?

What did your mother do that made you sad?

Describe how you are like your mother.

What do you wish you could tell your mother?

How did your parents show physical affection towards each other?

Did your parents spend time alone with each other?

Did you go on family vacations? If yes, where? Did you enjoy the family vacations?

Were your parents divorced?

How old were you when your parents divorced?

How did you feel when they divorced?

Describe your relationship with your sibling(s).

How much time do you spend with your sibling(s)?

What was the great gift your sibling(s) gave to you?

Does/Do your sibling(s) tell you that they love you?

What did your sibling(s) do that made you sad?

What did your sibling(s) do that made you happy?

What was your first job?

How old were you when you started working?

What do/did you like about your job?

What do/did you dislike about your job?

What is your most outstanding accomplishment on the job?

What is your biggest failure on the job?

Describe your typical day at work.

What type of relationships do/did you have with your co-workers?

What has been your most satisfying job and why?

What motivates you in your job?

Who is the best mentor you ever had and why?

Do you mentor anyone? If so, why do you mentor?

What is your ideal job and why?

What is your measure of success on the job?

What is your advice about working?

What is your advice concerning looking for a job?

Do your feel that you balance your job with your family life; with your spiritual life; and with your personal life?

What do you like to do in your free time?

What do you like about your free time activity?

How do you feel when you are doing your free time activity?

What brings you joy?

What makes you sad?

What inspires you?

What motivates you?

Have you ever been scared? If so, what scared you?

Do you ever feel like crying? Do you cry?

Have you ever laughed until you cried?

What angers you? How do you handle your anger?

Describe characteristics of a good friend.

What made you laugh the hardest?

What are your fondest memories of being with your friends?

What activities do you and your friends like to do and why?

What do you feel is the purpose of life?

What is your religion?

What do like about your religion?

How do you feel when you are practicing your religion?

What do you wish women would ask you?

What do you need from a woman?

What do you admire about women?

What do you dislike about women?

How do you feel connected to the Earth?

What is your fondest memory of being outdoors?

What do you like about animals?

Do/did you have a favorite animal?
Why?

Do/did you have a favorite pet? Why?

What is your favorite smell?

What is your favorite physical feeling?

What is your favorite noise?

What is your favorite sight?

What is your favorite taste?

Have you ever had a premonition?

Has your heart ever felt like it was breaking? What happened?

Do you have any regrets? If so what are they?

Describe what love feels like.

What concerns you about the world?

How would you like to be remembered?

What's your life code?

Why do you believe or not believe in God?

What about me most surprises you?

What's your earliest memory?

Who was your childhood hero?

Where did you go on your first date?

What made you successful at work?

What is the best advice your dad ever gave you?

www.ingramcontent.com/pod-product-compliance
Ingram Content Group UK Ltd.
Pitfield, Milton Keynes, MK11 3LW, UK
UKHW022016190726
13853UKWH00005B/1966

9 798531 489784